200 Easy Sight Reading Studies for Guitar

Key Signatures of C, G, F, D, Bb, A, Eb, and E Major.

All exercises are in 4/4 time, using simple rhythms. The book is arranged by key signature, and since each key signature begins at the same extremely easy level and progresses through its 25 exercises, you may work on any key signature in any order. When you have outgrown the 200 studies included in this book, I recommend moving on to my book:

1000 Music Reading Studies for Guitar

available at:

www.RobertAnthonyPublishing.com

Instructional video links will be posted at the above website as videos are produced. If this book is helping you, please post a positive review at whichever website you had purchased it from. If you have questions, suggestions, or constructive criticism, feel free to use the email link on my site to let me know.

over Art Citations: Can Stock Photo / David Schrader / colorvalley

Table of Contents

Classical Music Themes for Easy Guitar — Volume One — With Tablature — J.S. Bach, W.A. Mozart, Liszt, Chopin, Vivaldi, Haydn, Beethoven, Clementi, Schubert, Mendelssohn, Chopin, and many more. — Robert Anthony Publishing

Guitar Chords for the Singer-Songwriter and Beyond — Chords and Their Functions in a Musical Context — Robert Anthony

Whole, Half, and Quarter Notes
And How to Count Them in 4/4 Time

Whole Notes receive 4 beats:

Half Notes receive 2 beats:

Quarter Notes receive 1 beat:

Dotted Half Notes receive 3 beats

Instructional videos on rhythm and counting will be posted at www.RobertAnthonyPublishing.com as they are created.

Key Signature of C Major
Relative to A Minor

The six note range used in this section is below:

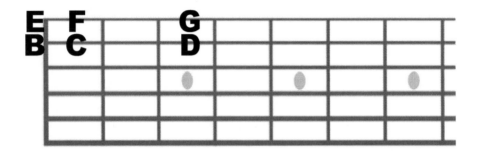

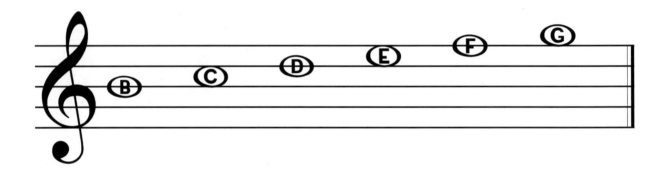

The exercises in this book may be played higher on the fretboard. To avoid confusion, the diagram uses the most common note-placement that a beginning guitarist would use. On the fretboard Diagram, the 6th string (lowest in pitch) is at the bottom of the diagram, while the 1st string (highest in pitch) is at the top of the diagram.

16

Key Signature of G Major
Relative to E Minor

The six note range used in this section is below:

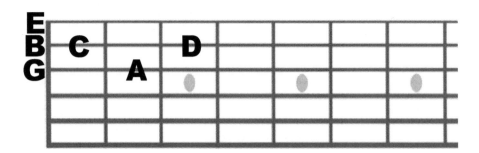

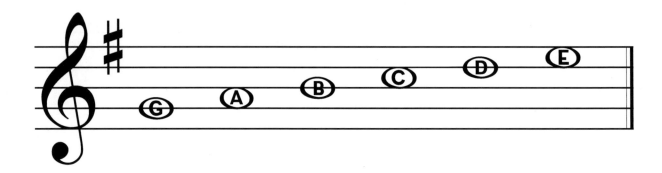

The exercises in this book may be played higher on the fretboard. To avoid confusion, the diagram uses the most common note-placement that a beginning guitarist would use. On the fretboard Diagram, the 6th string (lowest in pitch) is at the bottom of the diagram, while the 1st string (highest in pitch) is at the top of the diagram.

Key Signature of F Major
Relative to D Minor

The six note range used in this section is below:

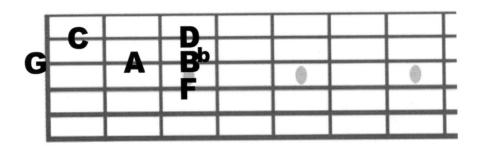

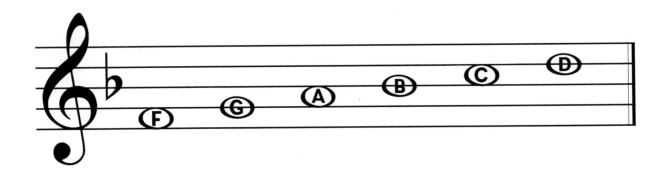

The exercises in this book may be played higher on the fretboard. To avoid confusion, the diagram uses the most common note-placement that a beginning guitarist would use. On the fretboard Diagram, the 6th string (lowest in pitch) is at the bottom of the diagram, while the 1st string (highest in pitch) is at the top of the diagram.

44

75

Key Signature of D Major
Relative to B Minor

The six note range used in this section is below:

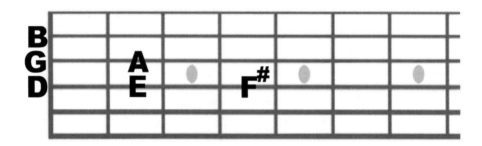

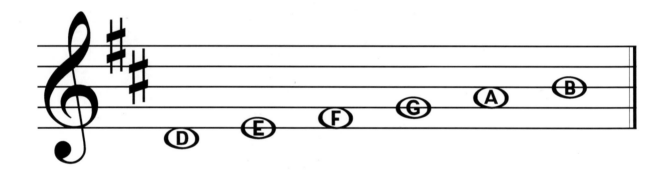

The exercises in this book may be played higher on the fretboard. To avoid confusion, the diagram uses the most common note-placement that a beginning guitarist would use. On the fretboard Diagram, the 6th string (lowest in pitch) is at the bottom of the diagram, while the 1st string (highest in pitch) is at the top of the diagram.

100

Key Signature of Bb Major
Relative to G Minor

The six note range used in this section is below:

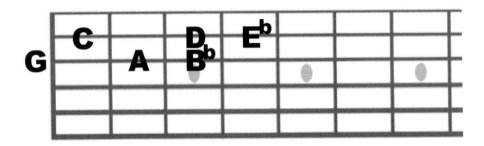

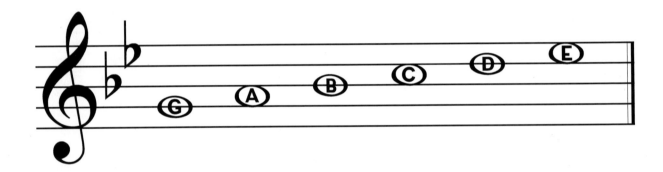

The exercises in this book may be played higher on the fretboard. To avoid confusion, the diagram uses the most common note-placement that a beginning guitarist would use. On the fretboard Diagram, the 6th string (lowest in pitch) is at the bottom of the diagram, while the 1st string (highest in pitch) is at the top of the diagram.

125

Key Signature of A Major
Relative to F# Minor

The six note range used in this section is below:

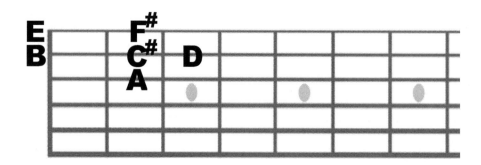

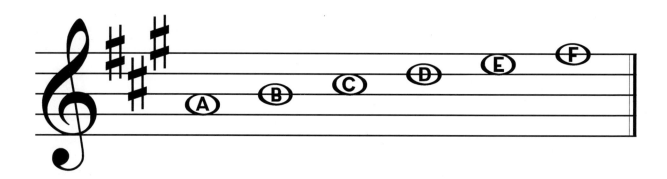

The exercises in this book may be played higher on the fretboard. To avoid confusion, the diagram uses the most common note-placement that a beginning guitarist would use. On the fretboard Diagram, the 6th string (lowest in pitch) is at the bottom of the diagram, while the 1st string (highest in pitch) is at the top of the diagram.

Key Signature of Eb Major
Relative to C Minor

The six note range used in this section is below:

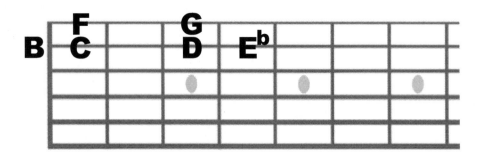

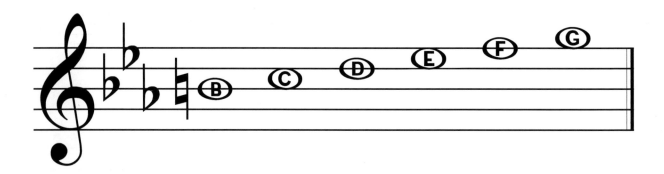

The exercises in this book may be played higher on the fretboard. To avoid confusion, the diagram uses the most common note-placement that a beginning guitarist would use. On the fretboard Diagram, the 6th string (lowest in pitch) is at the bottom of the diagram, while the 1st string (highest in pitch) is at the top of the diagram.

98

Key Signature of E Major
Relative to C# Minor

The six note range used in this section is below:

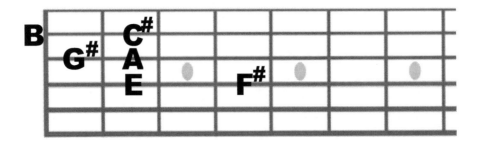

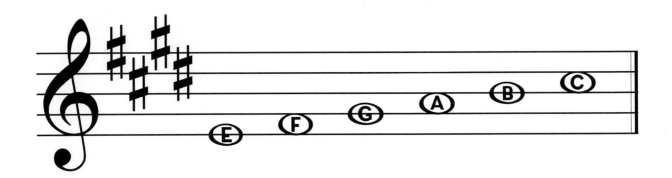

The exercises in this book may be played higher on the fretboard. To avoid confusion, the diagram uses the most common note-placement that a beginning guitarist would use. On the fretboard Diagram, the 6th string (lowest in pitch) is at the bottom of the diagram, while the 1st string (highest in pitch) is at the top of the diagram.

Glossary of Musical Terms

Adagio: slowly
Allegretto: fairly fast
Allegro: fast
Andante: moderately slow
Andantino: usually faster than andante
Animato: lively, animated
Cantabile: in a singing style
D.C. al Fine: repeat from the beginning until fine
Dolce: sweetly
Expressivo: expressively
FIne: the end
Grave: very slow, solemnly
Grazioso: gracefully
Lento: very slow
Mesto: sad
Moderato: Medium Tempo
Ritard: slow down
Très Expressif: very expressive
Vivace: lively
Waltz: in three

Dynamic Markings

Pianissimo ~ **pp**: very softy
Piano ~ **p**: softly
Mezzo Piano ~ **mp**: moderately soft
Mezzo Forte ~ **mf**: moderately loud
Forte ~ **f**: loud
Fortissimo ~ **ff**: very loud

Made in the USA
Columbia, SC
10 January 2025

51526793R00065